T0273385

Charlie Wheeller

One Million to STOP THE TRAFFIK

Adapted from Mark Wheeller's Play

Salamander Street

PLAYS

A previous version of this play was published by dbda (2010).

This edition published in 2022 by Salamander Street Ltd,
272 Bath Street, Glasgow, G2 4JR (info@salamanderstreet.com).

PB ISBN: 9781914228452

10 9 8 7 6 5 4 3 2 1

Further copies of this publication can be purchased from
www.salamanderstreet.com

One Million to STOP THE TRAFFIK Acknowledgements

Ruth Dearnley OBE, Bex Keer and Phil Lane whose words have provided the backbone of this play. Veronica's story – *STOP THE TRAFFIK: People shouldn't be bought and sold: The Crime That Shames Us All* – Steve Chalke. Lion Hudson Plc.

Veronica's story: ILO – IPEC Trafficking in Children 2005.

Cojo's story: Stories from the Ivory Coast owned by the International Labor Rights.

Kiri's story *(developed from an amalgam of trafficked peoples' experiences by Bex Keer).*

Jess from England is taken from *Stop! She's My Daughter (Mary's Story: What Price Justice? chapter)* © Christine Miles, 2007, a CROP publication *(Coalition for the Removal of Pimping).*

Mark Wheeller's Acknowledgements

Rachel and my family, who put up with my absence from home due to OYT enthusiasms.

STOP THE TRAFFIK for their ongoing support. Sam Allen Turner and her husband Richard of Avalon Entertainment Limited whose generous support allowed Oasis Youth Theatre to purchase the set and help raise the funds to get to Scotland to perform in the British Final. Sam (née Phillips) was a former OYT member. I'd like to thank her for remembering us!

Carley Wilson for administration support and a stream of ideas throughout the rehearsal period.

Kirsty Housley for her creative ideas during our one-day workshop.

Ian Golding, Principal, Oasis Academy Lord's Hill, for caring and active support throughout the development of this project.

Kate Bulpit, Business Development Director Oasis Academy Lord's Hill, whose tireless work fundraising allowed OYT to achieve what they did without worries.

John Cunningham at Central Oasis Press Team for PR work well beyond the call of duty.

Steve Chalke and all at Oasis Community Learning for support and much enthusiasm.

The cast of the original production and those who were part of the development team 2009/10.

Evie, Dawn & Lynda from dbda who were always so willing to consider my plays for publication.

George Spender and all in the Salamander Street team for valuing my plays and making the effort to help them extend their reach.

Sophie Gorell Barnes and all at MBA for their continued support and belief.

Charlie Wheeller for his involvement throughout this project and for his sensitive work on this new version of the script.

Mark Wheeller, 2022

Introduction by Mark Wheeller to his original *One Million to STOP THE TRAFFIK* (2010)

I had no idea that people in this day and age are still being bought and sold… let alone in such vast numbers. I had no idea until I witnessed a short, yet powerful presentation by STOP THE TRAFFIK in 2008. The campaign by this organisation had been established by the sponsors of the new Academy (Oasis) which had taken over our school that year. STT's presentation wanted to elicit ideas from staff for new projects. I had an idea, an awareness-raising documentary play.

I spoke to the presentation team and was allowed to progress the idea. I think they imagined a much smaller project than I had in mind. I was determined for them to see the quality of our work as early as possible, so asked them to send us some testimonies which I could give to my Oasis Youth Theatre team to work on. They kindly accepted my invitation to meet the cast and see these mini performances later that month.

By the time the testimony arrived I had assembled a group who quickly became excited by the potential of this play. We decided we would have an eighteen-month period to develop the play with performances planned for March 2010. It seemed a long way off and demanded much maturity from the cast with no instant performance reward.

The group was made up of fourteen old and new OYT members aged between fourteen and twenty-three. I purposely involved more people than I imagined would end up in the final production. The older ones were keen to break new ground with the production and use a more physical style of presentation than in previous Wheeller productions.

When I handed out the testimony (unaltered to small sub-groups) two groups independently decided to present the material using virtually no words. One of these scenes became the basis for what became our opening scene (Veronica's story) and set a style that we would use throughout.[1] The

---

1 This scene can be seen in its original form on the Wheellerplays – The Definitive Author's Collection DVD available as a streamed production from https://overture.plus/patron/Salamander-Street

three devisors/performers were hip-hop dancers. They cleverly and subtly incorporated 'popping' and 'waving' into their performance which I loved as soon as I saw it. This led us to the idea of portraying the predators with movement like this in the final production. We knew these scenes were special and couldn't wait to show Bex from STT. I remember driving her to the train station following the showing sensing she was beginning to see what potential our production might have.

I still didn't have a framework in which these stories could exist. I decided I didn't want to focus on one story because there were so many different forms of trafficking and I wanted the play to expose a range of them. I wanted to use the original testimony as it was so emotive. What I needed was a "guide" to tour the audience round the various problems. A visitor from Oasis Bangladesh came to the Academy and suggested that Phil Lane, who co-founded STOP THE TRAFFIK would fit the bill perfectly.

A meeting was set up, and following the Christmas break I interviewed Phil and I was able to start writing the script using his testimony.

Around that time, I also saw a TV film about the Labour party election victory under Tony Blair's leadership. It portrayed the climatic journey towards the majority he needed to win, and another idea struck me. STOP THE TRAFFIK's determination to obtain one million signatures could be interwoven with the harrowing testimonies of those trafficked. Thus, a structure was born and would also allow (with a bit of dramatic license) some light relief in what were to become the office scenes (now largely removed).

I remember arriving at our first meeting after the Christmas break with about half the script freshly photocopied. I left some lines unallocated (an idea I'd seen Mark Ravenhill use in his ensemble play *Pool No Water*) which allowed more flexibility in line allocation with this large cast. Such occasions are always nerve-wracking for me as I have no idea how my solitary efforts at home will be received. There was a very positive response and we immediately set about staging it using an original technique that offered maximum opportunity for everyone to have some input. It was simply for the group to "guess" where I intended them to go on stage at any given moment. They all had to remain actively involved. If they got completely stuck, they were allowed to talk which often led to more complicated ideas being developed.

The people in the office scenes did the same thing with Carley Sefton who organically took on the role of Assistant Director. At the end of the evening each group showed their work and benefited from forthright evaluations. These were sketches of the scenes just to check that they would work on stage. For the most part they did. I probably made fewer changes to this script in the rehearsals than any other I have worked on. From February to July, we continued in this manner knowing that in September rehearsals would begin.

We gave a short preview in July of the Veronica scene which is fascinating to look back on now. It can be seen on my *WheellerPlays – The Definitive Author's Collection* and shows the beginnings of the final scene which eventually had eighteen people in it! The version on the DVD was developed when I imagined we would have a much smaller cast and would only feature three OYT members. The obvious quality of this 'preview' served to raise expectations for *One Million to STOP THE TRAFFIK* as it was now entitled.

In September I created a new problem. I had met some young people during the year and I wanted to introduce them to OYT, added to the fact that fewer dropped out than anticipated so, we started rehearsals with a cast of twenty (it eventually went down to eighteen). Smaller casts generally fare better in the All England Theatre Festival we had decided to enter but we moved forward with the large cast in the blind faith that somehow it would work.

Stupidly, in retrospect we had failed to note down any of the movements we had developed in the previous school year and no one could remember what we'd done so we had to stage the play afresh from September. We used the "guess" technique for most of the play (Jess's scene was a notable exception as I wanted to do it very simply a la *Missing Dan Nolan* and have less people on stage). I was determined to incorporate the hip-hop dancers as puppeteer style predators throughout the play which meant they became central to the action but hardly ever spoke. It became the iconic idea of the production. It was so fortunate we had the talent in our group to pull it off so effectively!

By December we were able to show a complete run through to, amongst other interested parties, Bex from STOP THE TRAFFIK. This was a thrilling evening. The reaction was fantastic, even though for some scenes the cast were still working from scripts!

There was another development that evening. Our set designer had the idea of using a children's climbing frame. We'd been scouring catalogues to see if we could find something that would fit the bill with little success. Carley invited a set constructor friend (Chip) from the Nuffield Theatre to watch the preview. At the end I saw he was deep in conversation with the two predators and they came up with an idea of a custom-built steel frame.

The following week I was invited to see 3D designs for the proposed structure. Being perfectly honest I couldn't imagine how we could use this in the play. However, the cast had been so excited by the idea that I put my trust in them and commissioned it, spending literally all the donation money we had been given by a benefactor.

In January the structure arrived and using the basic moves for the production we'd shown to Bex, we re-rehearsed everything incorporating the new set. It was soon clear (even to me) what a major force this structure would become in the production. Our predators now perched on, hid in, and swung from the frame. It offered endless possibilities, fantastic use of levels and on some scenes the whole cast fitted inside it as though they were caged animals. The office scene transitions were sped up significantly by the simple addition of blocks on casters. It transformed what I already believed was a very impressive production.

Kat Chivers, our costume designer, designed simple but highly effective costumes. The ensemble wore black T-shirts (predators – red) with the STOP THE TRAFFIK 'key on hand' logo embossed on the front and on the back. A genius idea. A line from the script selected by each of the cast for their own shirt.

The next component was the original musical underscore OYT commissioned from ex-member Dave Jones which, with a more stable script, lifted each scene to ever increasing emotional heights. Danny Sturrock finally added his imaginative multi-media.

Everything was going so well then, ten days before the first performance... disaster! An overseas organization, who had provided a testimony, replied to a message Bex had sent months before withdrawing their permission for us to use one of the main stories in the play. Bex hoped we would be able to agree changes but could not offer me much reassurance that they would realise the urgency of the situation and speed up their communications.

I decided that the only way to move forward with ten days to go would be to completely replace the scene. I asked Bex to dictate over the phone a story that typified many different cases amalgamated to raise the issues the original story was aiming to raise. Forty-five minutes later I had a new story to adapt which I had written down hastily on whatever paper had come to hand! I spent the rest of the day adapting it for the rehearsal that evening. I went in and revealed the bad news. If we were to put the production on as planned we would have to plot this scene in this three hour rehearsal.

It was a nightmare but the crisis pulled us together and, by the end of the stressful evening, we felt we had possibly the most imaginative scene in the play… Kiri's scene.

The premiere was memorable. Phil Lane was there along with Steve Chalke who I had actually never met. I remember standing at the back of the Oasis Academy Theatre and noticing Steve, sat in the front row, looking at the programme during the early part of the play. I was concerned it wasn't holding his attention. Afterwards he told me that it was gradually dawning on him that this was the story he recognised and was using the program to check out that the Phil and Rachel who were on stage were the Phil and Rachel he knew. I imagine at that moment he would also have noticed that he too would soon be represented on stage. What a way to find out!

The reactions were unbelievable. We had a positive review from our local daily newspaper on the first preview but following the official premiere the Editor of the paper also gave over the main part of his weekly editorial to our production saying:

"Powerful, disturbing, emotional – it was one of the best productions I have seen in a long time, anywhere."

We couldn't believe how well it had been received. Well, actually we could… well… I could. I knew it was something very special.

Our production went on to win the All England Theatre Festival against 350 other competing adult and youth groups. We overturned the idea that only small-cast productions can do well at these festivals… quite an achievement as everyone in the cast had to be outstanding… and they were! We had the time of our lives representing England in Scotland for the British Final.

After this we went on to have the honour of performing it once more at Oasis' church in Waterloo in front of Cherie Blair and representatives from the United Nations who were flown in specifically to see our play! Not even I had imagined that!!!

All of us have been touched by the issues this play raised. We are all aware of what that fair trade logo means now and will make our consumer choices with a better understanding.

I'd like to end on a personal note. My own son, Charlie, has been in OYT for many years and this will (probably) be his final OYT production. He played the bongos offstage in his first ever production: *Missing Dan Nolan*. He has always been a committed member of OYT and won awards in each of the festivals he has participated in, most notably for being the bitch in the dog humping scene in *Race to be Seen!* In this production he was one of the hip-hop predators (along with Matt Savage) who created such a stir in every performance and also won a couple of awards. I shall miss our journeys together to and from Youth Theatre but I am so rewarded that he is now truly following his dream. He starts on a degree course in Circus Skills in the internationally renowned Circus Space (now The National Centre for Circus Arts) in London. It's a fabulous achievement to get a place on this prestigious degree course and I'm very proud that my son is running away to the circus!

Good luck to all of you who work on this production.

Mark Wheeller

Introduction by Mark Wheeller for the 2022 edition of *One Million to STOP THE TRAFFIK*

I am thrilled to be writing this and introducing you to Charlie (Wheeller) as a writer.

During the 2020 lockdown dbda, who published my original version of *One Million to STOP THE TRAFFIK*, unexpectedly closed their drama publishing arm and returned all the copyrights of my plays to me. This led to my partnership with Salamander Street, a new independent drama publisher. They wanted to take on almost all my back catalogue. *OMTSTT* was one play I was keen to be included.

I was determined that each of the Salamander Street Wheellerplays should have the chance of a new look so the new edition became genuinely worthwhile.

I contacted STOP THE TRAFFIK and established that I had only told a part of the STOP THE TRAFFIK story. Interestingly, I noticed today when re-reading my original introduction to this play that I wrote:

"A visitor from Oasis Bangladesh came to the Academy and suggested that Phil Lane, who co-founded STOP THE TRAFFIK would fit the bill (of narrating the story) perfectly."

I focused on the word *'co-founder'*.

I had never spoken to the other founder(s). I have no idea why, other than perhaps I was somewhat over-keen to have something ready for my eager cast to get working on.

I spoke to Bex Keer (who had since left STOP THE TRAFFIK) for the first time in ten years and she suggested I contact Ruth Dearnley. I had met Ruth while we were working on the play back in 2010 but I had never realised she was the CEO of STOP THE TRAFFIK!

I became aware that to include Ruth's story (which was a must) meant this was becoming a far bigger re-writing project than I could handle with a myriad of other re-writes already on the go!

Conveniently (to this story), Charlie had based himself back in our home during the lockdown and he had contributed to a few episodes of a

Wheellerplays Story YouTube project that I was doing to offer schools free resources which students could use at home.

Two of these were episodes about the OYT production of *One Million to STOP THE TRAFFIK* in which he had been a key part. I had no idea how he would react to my idea of him taking this on but I was aware he'd been enjoying some other writing.

Charlie enthusiastically took up the offer and we interviewed Ruth who provided us with this crucial part of the STOP THE TRAFFIK story.

At this point I bowed out and simply let Charlie 'get on with it'.

When I came to read the play, you now have in your hands, I was utterly delighted. It told the story well and highlighted the power of the women in this version.

I think Charlie and Ruth are already discussing a 'part two' to this play as so much has happened in the ensuing years. I look forward to seeing this come to fruition.

I have enjoyed taking a back seat and watching Charlie drive off with confidence to create a play that still has elements of my original but incorporates so much more.

Thank you Charlie for this development of a play which you came to know so well as a teenager. You were the perfect choice to undertake this revision. I knew you would have the passion to ensure it was looked after and improved.

Thanks also to Ruth for her inspiring words and to Phil for allowing us to move forward to tell this extended version of the STOP THE TRAFFIK story.

I can't wait to see it performed. I hope the world will soon be in a position to allow this to happen with a live audience. We are both looking forward to the proposed premiere in our home town of Southampton by the MAST Youth Theatre in 2023.

Very exciting times!

Mark Wheeller

Charlie Wheeller's Introduction

I had grown up watching my dad write and facilitate work that was, more often that not, allegorical. Sometimes, as with his fairytale on drugs *Wacky Soap* (now *Happy Soap*), it was more metaphorical, and other times, like *Missing Dan Nolan*, the educational side of it was brutally clear and went straight to the point; look after yourself, your friends and don't let them walk home alone in the dark. Symbolic theatre had been my early moral education; I was learning to see meaning in art.

Live performance was wonderful but the script, theatre encapsulated, fascinated me. It was a guidebook to make magic, like a musical score. Even better was that its success wasn't guaranteed which made it much more exciting to work with. As a family we would go to watch new versions of old plays and I would see how the same script could be played with, evolving its essence and bringing whatever fun to the mix that that company could offer. Alongside performing in local youth groups, I tried my hand at writing scenes and sometimes even full plays, coaxing my friends to rehearse and put them on with me. As a performer, I was drawn more to the physical side rather than the verbal and enjoyed these parts of the theatre world separately. Later in college my theatrical studies widened and I would come across companies like Frantic Assembly who opened me up to alternate ways of presenting scripts. In dance the theory of Labanotation intrigued me. How could one write down movement effectively and efficiently?

Since then my life has transformed dramatically as I ventured off to study at the National Centre for Circus Arts and, upon graduating in 2014, co-created an experimental acrobatic company, Barely Methodical Troupe. Flipping into the scene with our own brand of acrobatics mixed with tenderness and storytelling from the theatre world, BMT's three full-length shows have blasted across the globe. The Corona pandemic halted our tours and we were forced into an, honestly, welcome break. For the first time in seven years my Cyr Wheel (my circus specialty) and I stayed in one place, down in the South of England with my parents. Throughout touring, amongst other things, I would find time to read and write poetry. Here, in this new world where time was suddenly not a constraint, I treasured hopping between family time, spinning, reading and writing. My dad came to republish most of his catalogue and one, that I happened to originally be involved with, was asking for a rewrite. With much on his hands, and little in mine, he was gracious enough to let me take on the challenge. I loved revisiting this powerful play and am so excited for it to be taken on by large ensembles. Having re-interviewed and rewritten, as well as performing in it many times, I have a unique perspective on this script. I would like to share a little bit about those early stages of this play's creation and hopefully offer a little bit of insight into the 'character' that I took on.

In our first workshop for this new project, Dad provided us with a testimony about a trafficked girl, Veronica. We read it and we weren't really prepared for its intensity. It was a terrible story and we had no idea how to reenact it. Our cast was young, suited to play Veronica and other youth characters, but how do we portray those who trafficked her? How could we embody evil, the faceless violence that perpetrates these stories?

The scale and vision of this project had bought back some members from past productions and we were lucky enough to be in the presence of Matt Savage, one of the most savage body-poppers I had ever met. The group voiced ideas and then Matt started moving on his own trialing out something that had clearly come to him. We watched in awe as he started embodying his version of evil. Through his non-human-like movements he became a *Predator*. He threw away language and instead, would snarl and fight the air around him, furious arms reminiscent of Krump, destroying all that was in his path. My eyes widened and I was exhilarated by his terror. His movements drew you in, with their malicious motives, a perfect metaphor for these predators. Matt and I set to work with another magic mover, Becky Wiltshire, and together we started to choreograph Veronica's testimony, transposing the words to our bodies and setting it all to Bjork's enchanting song Joga. A couple of hours later we presented something and instantly the rest of the cast shared our vision. With the help of Stop The Traffik we gathered more stories like Veronica's and gave them the same 'savage' treatment.

My dad's work often deals with heavy issues and this was no different. As a youth group, you have to dig deep, mature fast and work out how you can make it 'fun' whilst still doing justice to the harrowing stories. Each bit of testimony requires its own sensitivities to draw out the realities of what the characters have been through. How do you make these injustices entertaining/informative/useful? These predators we had discovered, had empowered us to fight and create what became *One Million to STOP THE TRAFFIK*.

Charlie Wheeller

Introduction by *Ruth Dearnley OBE, CEO STOP THE TRAFFIK*

Telling stories is an important part of how we learn from our past and commit to changing things in the future.

STOP THE TRAFFIK's story started in 2005 and is still being written.

We are privileged to be working alongside Charlie and Mark Wheeller, who are great storytellers. Their commitment is to write a story that others can become a part of and bring it to life.

This piece of drama shares a moment in time, remembering across those STOP THE TRAFFIK early years, sharing the first chapter of how we got started, how we fought to be heard by gathering a million to build a movement committed to taking action.

Thank you to all those who have been part of bringing this project to life and here's to another million, writing themselves into the story, joining us to make a change & STOP THE TRAFFIK.

Ruth Dearnley OBE

CEO STOP THE TRAFFIK

Characters

In order of appearance:

PREDATORS

ANIMALISTIC SPIRITS/PUPPET-MASTERS IN CHARGE OF THE TRAFFICKING

VERONICA

A TRAFFICKED GIRL FROM MOLDOVA

KIRI

AN AMALGAMATION OF MANY DIFFERENT TRAFFICKED PEOPLE FROM ALL OVER THE WORLD.

COJO

A TRAFFICKED BOY FROM WEST AFRICA

YAO

A TRAFFICKED BOY FROM WEST AFRICA

JESS

A TRAFFICKED GIRL FROM THE UK

WHINNEY

TRAFFICKED FROM INDIA

SUNNI

TRAFFICKED FROM INDIA

RUTH DEARNLEY

CO- FOUNDER AND CEO OF STOP THE TRAFFIK

STEVE CHALKE

FOUNDER OF THE OASIS CHARITABLE TRUST AND A FORMER UNITED NATIONS SPECIAL ADVISER ON HUMAN TRAFFICKING

BEX KEER

UK TEAM MANAGER OF STOP THE TRAFFIK

PHIL LANE

*CO-FOUNDER OF STOP THE TRAFFIK
AND HUMAN RIGHTS ACTIVIST*

RACHEL

HUMAN RIGHTS ACTIVIST AND WIFE OF PHIL

PARENTS OF SUNNI AND WHINNEY

ALCOHOLIC COUPLE

MIKE

AN ENTHUSIASTIC FESTIVAL GOER

YOUNG PHIL

PHIL FROM THE PAST AT SCHOOL

MARY

MOTHER OF JESS

GEMMA

A TRAFFICKED GIRL FROM UK, FRIEND OF JESS

All the remainder of the cast play a variety of roles.

CAST LIST

Wednesday 10th March 2010 – Oasis Academy Theatre Lord's Hill, Southampton

PHIL LANE *Alex Chalk*

STEVE CHALKE *Michael Mears*

ALEX *Kathryn Wiltshire*

ERIN *Kylie Boylett*

ENSEMBLE

All the remainder of the cast play a variety of roles. I have indicated below the role that most easily distinguishes them in order of appearance:

VERONICA *Becky Wiltshire*

PREDATORS *Matt Savage & Charlie Wheeller*

YOUNG PHIL *Callum Watts*

RACHEL *Natasha Thomas*

SUNNI *Rob King*

WHINNEY *Hayley Willsher*

THEIR FATHER *Caidyn White*

KIRI *Lauren Oakley*

RAID LEADER *Joey Marks Reilly*

COJO *Kyle Nicholas*

MARY *Gemma Aked Priestley*

JESS *Kimberley Cook*

BACKSTAGE TEAM

DIRECTOR *Mark Wheeller*

ASSISTANT DIRECTOR *Carley Sefton-Wilson*

HEAD OF VIDEO *Danny Sturrock*

HEAD OF LIGHTING *Amy Barnett*

HEAD OF SOUND *Dave Jones*

HEAD OF COSTUME *Kat Chivers*

SET DESIGN/CONSTRUCTION *Charles "Chip" Mead from Laura Swale's original idea*

STAGE MANAGER *James Jones*

OYT ADMIN *Chris Gilfoy & Claire New*

LIGHTING OPERATION *Dan Phillips*

POSTER DESIGN *Danny Sturrock*

In the original version of One Million to STOP THE TRAFFIK, there were detailed music and media cues. Should you wish to explore the music/media commissioned for the original production (much of which could be useful) please contact Salamander Street who will facilitate this.

Preset: Although the play is divided into sections, when it is performed it should be performed seamlessly with no blackouts. N.B. Every opportunity should be taken to animate the scenes, to avoid the scenes becoming stationary talking heads.

The lines from X should be allocated by the performing group/director as suits each presentation, chorally or individually. The words themselves are sacrosanct as they are taken from interviews or original testimony.

Section One

INTRODUCTION

Lighting fades up to reveal a trafficked group, asleep in the middle of a messy stage, huddled together to keep themselves warm. **PREDATORS**, *behaving as vulture/vampire-like creatures, perch on a cold metal climbing frame structure upstage of the pile of bodies. Throughout the production they take control, puppeteer like, forcing the actions of the victims. Here they use their 'magnetic' power from their hand and lure their victims individually from their slumber, dotting them around the stage. They use dark body popping to simulate the animalistic nature of the* **PREDATORS** *and also to morph from one scene/location/ character to another.*

Each of the victims portrayed later in the play stand in silence rocking backwards and forwards awaiting their fate. Each recites their name and age to an imaginary interrogator.

VERONICA: Veronica. Moldova, sixteen.

KIRI: Kiri, from so many places in the world… fourteen.

COJO: Cojo.

YAO: … and Yao.

BOTH: West Africa. Thirteen.

JESS: Jessica. England. Thirteen.

WHINNEY: Whinney *(Pron. Viyernee.)*… nine and my brother.

SUNNI: Sunni… *(Pron. Sooni.)*

SUNNI AND WHINNEY: India.

ALL VICTIMS: Seven. *(Pause.)* We're here to work… aren't we?

> *One by one the victims are overpowered by the* **PREDATORS** *and forced back into a "prison" (where they form a frieze: Captivity) with the exception of the final victim,* **VERONICA** *who the* **PREDATORS** *surround.*

X: Veronica is sixteen years old. She was trafficked to Russia by a Roma family.

The scene transforms and **VERONICA** *mimes hoeing the land. A group enter as farmers, involving themselves in agricultural activities e.g. carrying a pot, hoeing, harvesting, working with oxen on a yoke etc. The victims in their frieze behind* **VERONICA** *make sounds expressing discomfort, underscoring the rest of the scene. Alternatively, this can be pre-recorded and played over the music. The* **PREDATORS** *do as the narration dictates.*

X: They promised her work in agriculture but she was forced to beg sitting in an invalid chair. To make her foot numb, the traffickers injected her.

VERONICA: *(She starts to beg.)...* Help... please... money... please...

Commuters pass by expressing a variety of reactions: laughing, ignoring her, on occasions offering her money. The commuters leave. The **PREDATORS** *return.*

X: They forced her to take drugs and drink alcohol.

VERONICA: Drugs... alcohol ... alcohol... drugs... Veronica... sixteen.

The **PREDATORS** *slam her to the ground and shout.*

PREDATORS: Beg.

They chorally mime beating her and ensnare her. When she is settled, they make disturbing vocal sounds denoting they fall asleep.

X: Veronica was exploited for three months earning 400 lei which amounts to about thirty pounds.

X: *(Whispering from those in captivity.)* Go! Just go! Get out of here... freedom, run!

VERONICA *attempts to escape twice.*

X: *(Whispering.)* Go! Just go! Get out of here... freedom, run!

On the third attempt she evades her captors. She exits. The **PREDATORS** *angrily turn to blame each other then exit to search for* **VERONICA**, *who re-enters and runs into the STOP THE TRAFFIK team who arrive onstage with backpacks and bags. One predator enters and, seeing she is now with others, backs off frustrated.*

Section Two

BEGINNINGS

Throughout this next scene, the STT team start unpacking and fixing the space behind **RUTH***, like it hasn't been used for a while. The litter on the stage is repurposed as personal decoration. They turn on small lamps and redress the space to make it feel warmer. From bags, they get out files and folders with papers, laptops and other 'work' paraphernalia. Gradually,* **STEVE** *and* **BEX** *join* **RUTH** *in telling their story to the audience.* **PHIL***'s attention is taken by a distressing casefile he's found upstage. He remains immersed until he is called upon. Throughout the play, more and more ensemble members join in with these scenes, showing STT's reach growing. They assist them, becoming useful and playing other characters whenever required. By the end of the play, every cast member seems to be part of the STT office team.*

RUTH: You know, when they announced to put a man on the moon they had no idea they could do it. That's an incredible statement really, but they were far enough along to think they could, and I suppose that's where we're at in stopping the traffik. *(Introducing herself.)* Ruth.

STEVE: Steve.

BEX: Bex.

PHIL: Phil.

RUTH: Back in 2005…

STEVE: …whilst Ruth and I were leading a team working on another project…

RUTH: …Steve said something around trafficking one evening, over a glass of wine.

STEVE: We were approaching the anniversary of the abolition of slavery. 200 years since William Wilberforce's bill…

RUTH: And he said, "Why don't you do that with me?" And I said, "alright then." That really was the shortest interview I've ever had and the most profound. But little did I ever know you don't do those things knowing where it's going. You do those things because there's a call in you, an urge in you, to want to be involved.

STEVE: From that evening, one of our team is a wordsmith poet…

A member of the ensemble quickly volunteers to play this part, peppered with smugness. This poet assumes they will say these lines and perhaps even read their pivotal poem. But **STEVE** *stays on script and doesn't even notice them.*

STEVE: …and the following day they came down and said, "I've got a name, got a name for what you're going to do" and they wrote a poem.

Disappointment from the poet.

STEVE: And from there, STOP THE TRAFFIK was born. We became volunteers and Bex, the only paid employee, became the administrator.

BEX: And what we did in that first, I'd say, six months is; we began to bring in organizations, mainly from Ruth and Steve's Christian networks, where trafficking was already becoming… just starting to come onto their radar.

RUTH: Two had trafficking on their agenda. Salvation Army and Oasis. Oasis was a Global Charity that worked with some of the world's poorest and most marginalised communities. Steve set it up.

STEVE *waves serendipitously.*

RUTH: Oasis had already started to see this through and… with Salvation Army – well their ability to see things on the ground, is bar none. So they had stories, they were doing work.

STEVE: Banks and businesses are now starting to engage in stopping traffiking too – they're not all asking the right questions, lots are still looking for that gold bullet, 'let me find the baddie and arrest them', they're still stuck in the past.

RUTH: But actually together, we can get the stories, turn them into insight and democratize that to everyone who can make the maximum change. There's something very powerful in that, "look there's our goal", because if we don't, we don't give any of the generation behind us any access…because *you* have to lead this next ten years just as much. There was a story with Whinney and Sunni.

PHIL'*s ears prick up. She ushers him over.*

RUTH: We articulated Phil as being very much at the founding moment, because of what he saw on that station platform in Mumbai.

PHIL: To cut a long story short, after uni I got a leaflet offering the opportunity to do some voluntary work overseas so I found myself working for Oasis Global Charity and … I met my wife Rachel.

Section Three

MUMBAI

RACHEL: I was also on a placement in Mumbai, India!!

X: A city of about eighteen million people…

ALL: Eighteen million?

PHIL: … and thousands of street kids.

RACHEL: We set up a drop-in centre on Thane *(pron. Tarner)* railway station.

X: It's a medium sized station… about eight or nine platforms…

X: … people live there begging…

X: … doing menial jobs…

X: … getting chased…

X: … by the police…

X: … sleeping on the roofs.

X: Everyone comes into Thane Station.

X: Kids come in from all over rural India looking for the streets paved with gold in Mumbai…

RACHEL: … they've seen the Hindi movies…

PHIL: … they know that's where it's all made…

X: … their parents migrate there in the hope of work…

X: … then…

X: … the kid gets lost…

PHIL AND RACHEL: …or… the parent dies of AIDS.

Silence.

RACHEL: We got to know those kids and set up a drop-in centre for them.

PHIL: Sounds like a grand name… for what it was.

X: Two small buildings…

X: … with a gap between them.

RACHEL: We asked the owner to put a roof on the gap.

PHIL: That was our drop-in centre.

RACHEL: We used to get forty kids packed in there.

X: They'd teach literacy.

X: Numeracy.

X: Life skills.

X: And games such as:

ALL: Cricket!

PHIL: Giving them room to be kids…

RACHEL: …cos they spend their whole time trying to earn money.

X: Trying to avoid the police…

X: …or being beaten up by gangs.

PHIL: Somewhere safe with food and time to enjoy themselves.

RACHEL: We started a night shelter.

PHIL: There's a hardcore who sleep on the station… alone.

RACHEL: That's who we were aiming at.

PHIL: At the beginning the shelter was just for boys.

RACHEL: Girls were always controlled by somebody – a family member or a pimp or whatever.

PHIL: That was when we started to realise about the exploitation of girls.

X: There was a growing fear of HIV in early 2000s.

PHIL: There was a myth that spread quicker than the virus:

X: "If you are HIV positive and you have sex with a virgin you lose the infection."

PHIL: So, there was a growing trade with younger and younger girls…

X: … and sometime boys…

RACHEL: … being forced into prostitution.

ALL: And *(Pause.)* there was the sale *(Pause.)* of children.

*As **SUNNI** and **WHINNEY** introduce themselves, their parents are on the floor behind them, drunk seemingly unconscious. Before **PHIL** and **RACHEL** talk to their **FATHER**, their **MOTHER** wakes up and skulks off looking for something. She doesn't acknowledge her children. She re-enters once she hears arguing.*

SUNNI: Brother

WHINNEY: … and sister.

SUNNI: Sunni…

WHINNEY: … and Whinney. *(Pron. Viyernee.)* Whinney was about nine.

SUNNI: … and Sunni was about seven.

BOTH: They lived on Platform 1 of Thane station with their…

Look back at their parents, disappointed.

BOTH: …Mum and Dad.

PHIL: Dad was particularly unpleasant…

RACHEL: Sunni and Whinney were just kids.

WHINNEY: They used to come along and play…

SUNNI: … and be annoying.

PHIL: You'd give them a meal and they'd complain about it…

RACHEL: … you know just the way it should be in some ways.

SUNNI AND WHINNEY: They were full of play and joy and would march out in umbrage…

PHIL AND RACHEL: …but… one day… they didn't come back.

SUNNI: Street kids often disappear for one or two weeks…

WHINNEY: … get on the long-distance trains…

SUNNI: … sweep the trains or sell things and take the money.

RACHEL: We thought they'd done that…

PHIL: … but after a week or so… when they didn't return, we went looking for their parents.

RACHEL: It was early morning… about 10 o'clock. We found their dad…

FATHER: … drunk and lying on the floor.

PHIL: I speak some Hindi but we also work with great Indian staff who translate for us!

An ensemble member quickly joins to become the translator.

RACHEL: For speed we'll lose the translators in this reconstruction!

Quick disappointment and quick exit from the translator. **PHIL** *and* **RACHEL** *awake the* **FATHER***, he is baffled.*

PHIL: "We haven't seen Sunni and Whinney for a week or so… do you know where they are? Have they gone on the trains?"

FATHER: No. This man offered me fifteen hundred rupees for them.

PHIL: That's just £20!

FATHER: I was thirsty… so I sold them!

PHIL: Do you have any idea where they've gone?

FATHER: No.

PHIL: Don't you care?

FATHER: Of course, I care! The bastard walked off with my kids but didn't give me my bloody money!

RACHEL: How can you say that?

FATHER: They're only children!

RACHEL: Do you have any idea where they are?

PHIL: Do the police know?

RACHEL: The wife was a few metres away and she was kind of glaring at him.

PHIL: I got the impression she didn't want it to happen but she couldn't stop it.

RACHEL: She'd lost all kind of influence or self-control or whatever because she was constantly drunk! At that point we went off to find the railway police to see if we could track them down.

PHIL: I know the parents come over VERY badly in this story and they did an incredibly awful thing but, what's happened to them in their lives, they've totally lacked all the support and the love and the sense of their self-worth that we've had, all the way through our lives so… well… they had no standard of care to measure their decisions against.

RACHEL: If we could have got the money for them they would have thought that was fantastic… or even better…

BOTH PARENTS: …booze!

PHIL: Oasis now has a good relationship with the police at a city level but back then there was no mechanism for persuading them to take action.

WHINNEY: What happened to Whinney and Sunni?

RACHEL: Nobody knows.

SUNNI: Kidnapped and sold into prostitution?

WHINNEY: Forced labour?

SUNNI: Adoption?

PHIL: … or even *(Pause.)* child sacrifice.

RACHEL: The story was passed on…

PHIL: … and, as evidence gathered, we realized this was happening on a huge scale.

RACHEL: This wasn't just Mumbai, it was across India.

PHIL: This wasn't just India, it was Asia.

X: This wasn't just Asia…

X: … it was across the world.

RACHEL: It's not 200 years ago.

X: Not even fifty years ago.

X: It was…

X: … and is still…

X: … happening today.

PHIL: We left India and came to take a position for Oasis in Europe… well I did.

RACHEL: Me? I decided to take a back seat, as I was busy being a full-time mum while Phil started to campaign on human trafficking.

*They share a look, almost a private joke, and **RACHEL** sweetly waves and exits.*
***PHIL** turns to address **STEVE** who enters from the opposite side of the stage.*

Section Four

CHOCOLATE

PHIL: There's millions of Sunnis and Whinneys, but people don't know about it.

STEVE: Millions?

PHIL: Between one and two million every year!

STEVE: How do you know?

PHIL: It's like asking for proof of the number of domestic abuse victims. Most are hidden. I can't prove a figure. The US State Department estimate nearly a million people are trafficked across borders each year… kids are trafficked to fight for the military and some… some are even trafficked for their internal organs. Steve… we can't do this on our own.

They draw closer to each other and brew together, shooting for the moon. **RUTH** *enters downstage and addresses the audience directly.* **BEX** *joins the background scene, answering a phone call, and other ensemble members gradually join their ship. It is a lively, cooperative environment.*

RUTH: In those first few years, you could see all these streams of engagement, a lot of engagement, in education, in inspiration, in moving people, in action, you know, there was all this that creates, doesn't it, if you give it away enough, a global sense of people being able to say "I can join in", "I can do this", "I can do that"… you know, we were enabling people not to ever be motivated by guilt but by empowerment.

A eureka moment in the background scene.

BEX: Chocolate!

RUTH: Chocolate became an iteration of what Wilberforce had done, his boycott. He did it with sugar, Ghandi did it with salt, so we were just mirroring – chocolate.

STEVE: We've all got power to make a difference, if we even just change the chocolate that we buy. We came up with various campaign's aiming at specific businesses.

X: Wrap up your favourite Fair Trade chocolate bar...

X: ... and send it to (the chocolate company) Nestlé with a lovely Christmas message.

X: We're wrapping up Fair Trade chocolate for Christmas presents...

STT: ... shame it's not yours!

PHIL: We called for fondue parties, suggesting people...

X: ... to dip all sorts of things in slavery-free chocolate and then send them to specific companies.

RUTH: I remember coming into the office once and Bex and I... she was in hysterics, she had a picture of what people had dipped into their fondue in Albania, it was very, very different.

BEX: We created a script for another of our campaigns:

X: March on Mars.

RUTH: We listed the different chief executives of Mars in every country, and people could ring them up and ask them when their Mars will be traffik-free!

BEX: We got a great conversation where someone rang up and said, "you know you're gunna love this, I just rang Mars and they said:

X: *(Stuffy impersonation.)* "Well we're not sure but if you phone STOP THE TRAFFIK, they seem to know quite a lot!"

Everyone enjoys this story.

Beat.

The ensemble gradually creates Sikasso bus station as **RUTH** *speaks. It is a busy station, reminiscent of the platform at Thane.*

RUTH: It isn't actually about what it is, chocolate... it's the others watching. Business is watching. Business is saying that "whatever happened to the chocolate industry is coming our way." And we have to stick at this so we have to create the change and of course, we saw the chocolate companies begin to make declarations. You know, we were exhausted, we weren't getting anywhere but we kept going, we kept going innovating different campaigns. *(To her colleagues.)* The first ones who went were Cadburys, weren't they?

X: Cadburys are going to make an announcement this afternoon… it is due to your campaign but they won't say it.

RUTH: And then we had the same with… it was Mars that went next and then Nestlé. *(Laugh.)* I won't stop until we have achieved something. Announcements aren't enough. Action, action, action!

Section Five

COJO

*STEVE walks amongst the scene trying to retain his anonymity and finds a place to wait and watch, mulling something over with a pen in hand. The ensemble become the 'workers' of the farm and they don linen ponchos, reminiscent of the sacks of cocoa they must carry. Throughout the next scene, **STEVE** reaches and interrupts some of the 'workers' and offers them a pen to draw a key in their hand. Each are initially reluctant to speak to **STEVE** but once they draw their key of freedom, they take off their poncho and join **STEVE**. We only realise what they have been drawing at the end when **STEVE** outstretches his hand.*

STEVE: In West Africa, boys are trafficked to work on cocoa farms. Agents hang around bus stations looking for children, such as Cojo *(**COJO** enters),* who are alone or begging for food.

COJO: I left home to earn money for my family. When I got to Sikasso bus station, I… *(**COJO** looks around the bus station.)* … I knew no one.

X: What is your name?

COJO: Cojo Sir.

X: Looking for work Cojo?

COJO: Yes.

X: I take you to my brother.

COJO: He has work?

X: Yes.

COJO: Here?

X: The Ivory Coast.

COJO: I have come to work in Sikasso. My father has died. I must stay near my mother.

X: Work here pays badly.

X: Cojo, come with me to Korgho.

COJO: No.

X: You will make lots of money.

COJO: Thank you sir but I stay here to work.

X: My brother pays very well. Will be good for your poor mother?

COJO: I am too small to go there.

X: They give you good food.

X: Chicken…

X: … Coca Cola.

COJO: Sir! I am only ten!

X: Finally the agent drove Cojo to the Ivory Coast.

COJO: I was actually excited by how much it would help mother.

X: They avoided the border control.

COJO: Once across the border I was completely alone. I was taken to a warehouse to sleep. The man who brought me disappeared. There are many children in the warehouse, sometimes more than one hundred. The cocoa planters come and see the warehouse owner. I hear them negotiating my sale.

X: Twelve.

X: Seven.

X: Eleven.

X: Eight.

X: Ten.

X: Nine. Sold!

COJO: Then I'm taken to the plantation.

*A **PREDATOR** reveals many sacks of beans from under a cloth. The 'workers' stare at their mission, already defeated.*

COJO: One job was to transport the cocoa beans. The bags were taller than me.

X: People placed the bags onto Cojo's head.

X: They were so heavy he often fell down.

X: The farmer beat him till he stood up to lift the bag.

COJO: We worked from six in the morning to about ten at night. We'd sit on the ground picking up cocoa pods with one hand and, with the other, hacking them open with machete to scoop out the beans.

X: Common injury with machete was cutting…

X: … or accidental amputation *(animate this with a choral quick empathetic intake of breath)* on the hands.

X: Open wounds expose the boys to HIV.

X: Applying pesticides without the necessary protective equipment leads to horrific skin burns and respiratory damage.

X: These can be fatal.

COJO: If we refuse to work the plantation owners bring razors and slice our feet.

X: They put salt in the wounds.

STEVE: The children have no communication with anyone.

COJO: One boy I knew, Yao, tried to escape.

STEVE: The plantations are isolated… in the middle of forest. There are no roads out… just fields everywhere.

YAO: They tied him to a papaya tree. They beat him.
They broke his arm.

STEVE: The pleasure that people from various nations around
the world derive from chocolate could be at the expense of children
trafficked and enslaved to harvest cocoa beans. This must <u>stop!</u>

STEVE *outstretches his hand and we see a key, the same key he has been drawing
on the hands of the 'workers'.*

Section Six

PETITION

RUTH: I think the minute I saw the hand, it felt right, because the hand was about human uniqueness, you know, you're looking at the fingerprints, the way, the way it was, every single human being is unique and valuable and that, in essence, is a principal that drives us. When it was produced it, it also looked like 'stop', there was a force to it. It wasn't a passive hand because the strength of human beings is that we have the ability to say stop, for others but also to empower people to say it for themselves. So, it's not about "I am here to rescue everyone", it's about the power for an individual to realize that…

X: …my uniqueness says that you must stop.

X: …my uniqueness says that you must stop.

X: …my uniqueness says that you must stop.

Comforting looks of encouragement are shared across the stage.

RUTH: Time was ticking, the campaigns were working, but we were still searching for something else… something big.

ALL: *(Melodramatically.)* Suddenly… there was a knock at the door!

X: *(Entering.)* Package. Can you sign here, please?

All four rush to sign.

X: I only need one; it's not a bloody petition.

They exit.

PHIL: *(Realising.)* A petition!

RUTH & STEVE: A petition!

BEX: It'll certainly raise awareness…

STEVE: We can gauge the level of interest.

PHIL: And those who sign feel they've done something about it.

RUTH: An easy way for anyone to take part in the…

ALL: "Global fight to STOP THE TRAFFIK".

STEVE: We do need a target…. something to aim for… a recognised number… recognised worldwide!

PHIL: Like what?

RUTH: 100,000?

BEX: *(Laughing.)* How will we get 100,000 signatures?

STEVE: No.

PHIL: It might be possible Steve.

BEX: *(Still laughing incredulously.)* Phil, it'd be 25,000 people each how are we gonna do that? I'm not sure I could find twenty-five!

PHIL: We can't give up so easily!

STEVE: We need a million!

Silence.

PHIL, RUTH AND BEX: A million?

STEVE: Yes. One million signatures to STOP THE TRAFFIK! That can't be ignored!

ALL: *(Melodramatically.)* A short while later…

The STT team move into a new position on stage to denote the passage of time. They bump into each other and acknowledge the "mistake" by saying each other's names, perhaps shaking hands in recognition of the error. Once in their new positions the scene reconvenes as though nothing has happened.

STEVE: *(Excitedly.)* We now have permission to go to the UN and call on governments to fight trafficking…. but only… if we get one million signatures.

PHIL: When?

STEVE: March 2007.

RUTH AND BEX: That's less than a year away.

STEVE: We can do it… I know we can. Come on… events… events where lots of people all gather together!

A moment's thought.

ALL: Glastonbury…

PHIL: There'll be loads of people there.

RUTH: Yeh… great place to start!

BEX: And I've already got a ticket!

PHIL: Perfect!

BEX: Have I just volunteered?

A busy scene is established… Glastonbury. We see **BEX** *in amongst the chaos with a clipboard trying and failing to start a conversation with some of the punters. Finally she manages to get someone's attention.*

BEX: Hi… my names Bex… I'm from Oasis…

X: Oasis?

BEX: Yes… Oasis… it's a global charity…

X: Ah right… sorry…. thought you meant "Oasis"… See ya!

A punter is having a wee in a corner. **BEX** *approaches them.*

BEX: Hi… I was wondering if I can have a moment of your time… my name's Bex…

X: Mine's Mike…

A moment of confusion from **BEX.** **MIKE** *offers his hand to shake.* **BEX** *pretends not to notice and continues the prepared script.*

BEX: I'm from STOP THE TRAFFIK…. basically kids from all over the world are being trafficked into slavery, and we want to get a million signatures.

MIKE: Oh I see.

BEX: All I need from you is a signature… and you'll be helping us to STOP THE TRAFFIK.

MIKE: Sure. *(**MIKE** signs.)*

BEX: Thanks very much.

Scene snaps back to the office. **RUTH** *is sat alone working in lamplight.*

RUTH: How many did you get… a thousand?

BEX: No.

RUTH: More or less?

BEX: One hundred and ninety-three. Look it was wet and people just wanted to…

RUTH: … it's a start.

BEX: One hundred and ninety-three out of a million?

RUTH: At least we don't have to get a million now!

Beat.

RUTH: The sad thing in life is everyone thinks that if they want to change something, they can do it fast, and you can't. Actually the secret is to keep running, it's like Forrest Gump isn't it?

BEX *snuffs a chuckle, not persuaded.*

RUTH: Steve… Steve told this story first and I just copied him. Steve and I went to America, in New York and we came out and we stood at… on the steps of Grand Central Station and literally, it was a spring day… I can't remember when but I had my dress on… I never wear dresses but we'd been to the UN you know. And the clouds came, the clouds gathered, it suddenly became really dark and it began to snow. Flakes came down and as they hit the ground they would just, because of the subway, they would disappear, from the heat on the street. And then, within twenty minutes, flakes, rivers, torrents, and the sky was completely white, I mean it was a snowstorm as I now know happens in spring in New York until the whole of the road was white and the traffic stopped.

BEX*'s body smiles.*

BEX: Is that where the… that's what helped you come up with… that's a great story. I did have a good idea while I was on the way home though.

RUTH: What?

BEX: The internet… there are groups on that for all sorts of mad stuff… thousands sign up to be a part of all sort of things.

The ensemble enact the actions of the groups mentioned.

BEX: Extreme Ironing,

Badly stuffed animals,

Accomplishing something before the microwave reaches 00…

One ensemble member completes a complicated task within an allotted time period and finish proudly.

RUTH: Hmm, bit silly.

Back to the petition at hand.

RUTH: I'm sure if that gets people to sign up then something like 'One Million people to STOP THE TRAFFIK' could do really well. Can you set it up?

BEX: Easy.

BEX *returns to the desk and gets to work.* **RUTH** *gathers her thoughts and addresses the audience.*

RUTH: I think for me, I don't know how to say this, I certainly couldn't see, I would never have imagined we'd have got to where we are, but what I did know is; I had to keep running because every time I ran around a corner you saw something else that helped you run more.

Section Seven

KIRI - FROM SO MANY PLACES

KIRI *is crying. Her sobbing becomes uncontrollable.*

X: Kiri's mother passed away.

X: People comfort her…

X: … and care for her…

X: … but one or two male figures in her community are not respectful.

    MAN 1 *approaches and starts to comfort her. They hug.*

KIRI: I miss my mum so much.

MAN 1: I miss her too Kiri… you must not cry my sweet… really… she wouldn't want that now would she…

The supportive hug becomes intrusive. It is clear he is beginning a journey towards rape. She screams. The scene freezes. He exits.

X: Kiri is alone…

X: … vulnerable.

X: And with a life changing decision to make.

X: To stay…

X: … or to leave.

X: Her friend tells her of an opportunity she'd be stupid to miss.

X: My sister has a job as a seamstress in the capital. You'd earn money Kiri. It would be good for you.

KIRI: I don't want to leave my family.

X: It is your only way to escape this hell! Go Kiri… be away from this place.

As they say this, the ensemble morph into a train.

KIRI: She boards a train determined to make something of her life. However, the job does not materialise. Kiri is alone… and vulnerable.

MAN 2: She meets a man… *(Ensemble simultaneously whisper these three words as she says them.)*…a kind man.

KIRI: Kiri feels secure… cherished.

The **PREDATORS** *suddenly restrain* **KIRI**.

MAN 2: *(Furious.)* Suddenly the charm disappears. *(***KIRI** *being held allows him to take her passport.)* He steals her passport. *(To* **KIRI**.*)* "If you go to the police they'll put you in prison. If you want to stay here you must pay for the food I give you."

KIRI: You know I have no money!

GIRLS: Kiri is sold to a man and moved…

BOYS: … to a "house"…

GIRLS: … where there are other girls.

X: The abuse begins.

Everyone, saying "Yes" lift her off the ground in a horizontal position.

X: They beat her and gave her electric shocks…

As they say this, there is a flash of light and she is lifted as high as possible and returned to a resting place.

X: … and drugged her.

KIRI: Which made her incoherent and compliant.

X: Some days she is forced to see up to ten men.

X: *(The predators force* **KIRI** *to smile by pulling her lips up with their fingers.)* Smile it'll be over soon.

KIRI: She feels foolish…

GIRLS: … guilty and ashamed.

KIRI: Isolated in a country where she doesn't speak the language. Kiri loses hope. A charity hears rumours of the brothel Kiri works in. They investigate.

X: They plan…

ALL: …and for once there is no tip off.

A simple movement sequence indicates an attack on the "establishment".

X: With the help of the police, Kiri and many of the other girls are rescued.

KIRI: I have the chance of a new life. I don't know what it will look like… but I have choices now. I can make good choices.

Section Eight

OFFICE- FINAL PUSH

PHIL *introduces* **YOUNG PHIL.**

PHIL: I was born in Coventry to a very stable, loving family. I was bullied a lot at school between the ages of – I guess when I started school, until I left Coventry at ten. Yes… perhaps that kicked off a hatred of unfairness… a lot of taunting…

X: Lanky!

PHIL: … being laughed at… *(Everyone points and laughs at* **YOUNG PHIL**.*)* I'll tell you something else that happened there as well. It was just when people from the Indian sub-continent were starting to come to the Midlands. There was one little girl from Bangladesh, Japinda, who could hardly speak English and the class mocked her dreadfully. I remember thinking it was so wrong.

X: But you didn't do anything about it?

X: What could he do?

X: Said something!

X: What would that do?

X: Get it "out there"!

ALL: No one listens to little kids.

PHIL: I remember trying to smile at her but she wasn't allowed to smile at a boy, and it's like… that feeling of isolation. I must have been about eight years old. Maybe that started it. I really haven't thought about it too much in a linked way. It was just the way the world was, but it did make me feel unhappy.

YOUNG PHIL: You can make a difference.

X: When you're eight?

YOUNG PHIL: Yes.

X: Not on your own!

YOUNG PHIL: *(To older* **PHIL.***)* You can and you will!

    YOUNGER PHIL *exits.*

RUTH: Every week we'd hear new stories, gather new information, it kept us moving forward

PHIL: ...but after a while the Facebook signatures plateaued...

BEX: At about 45,000.

PHIL: It seemed like... well... we'd tried everything.

RUTH: A million is such a big number.

BEX: Yes, do you know how long it takes to count to a million? Twenty-three days!

RUTH: How do you know that?

BEX: In one of my kid's books... twenty-three days! Just think how long it'll take to get a million signatures...

PHIL: There's no way we can do this.

BEX: Can it be less than a million?

STEVE: *(Entering the office.)* One million is the number that opens the door! We can only present our petition at the UN if we get one million signatures!

PHIL: It's very, difficult to get that level of interest... and getting signatures from undemocratic countries... Steve, these people don't want to draw attention to themselves.

STEVE: In this office there's always been a crazy optimism that we will find a solution. I don't want that to change. There's a million grains in a cup of salt. A cupful of signatures? We can do that!

RUTH: There's another problem. Middle class Europeans seem to think... well...

STEVE: ... this is all so far away?

RUTH: Yeah.

STEVE: We have to change that perception.

PHIL: Because it isn't.

X: It's right on our doorstep.

Section Nine

JESS FROM ENGLAND

PHIL: Mary Rogers' thirteen-year-old daughter was groomed and sexually exploited by a group of men.

JESS: Jess was born with a rare skeletal disorder that affects bone development.

MARY: As she got older, it became more noticeable that one arm was shorter.

JESS: I feel ugly mum. No lad I like will fancy me!

MARY: She wouldn't go out without a jacket, even if it was scorching, so, I was really proud of her when she became a majorette. One of my proudest moments was when her team won first prize at a holiday camp. She couldn't have looked any happier. Jess was a normal teenager in every other way; we had no problems at school. At weekends she went out with her friends but was always in on time. Once or twice I found out she'd had a drop of cider or something, and grounded her for a couple of nights, but you expect that. One Friday night in July 2005 however, she didn't come home.

JESS: See you Mum.

They give each other an "insignificant" kiss goodbye. **JESS** *exits.*

MARY: 10pm came and went. At 11.30pm I rang round her friends, then the police. I rang my ex-husband too and we went out to look for her. That was the worst night of my life. We searched the next day too. Then the police called.

X: "Jessica has been found, with a friend, Gemma".

GEMMA: Gemma was in foster care.

MARY: What I didn't know was Gemma was being groomed by a network of men operating across towns in England. Over the next few months, life became a nightmare. She wasn't washing and had… she had bruises and… love bites… all over. I didn't know her anymore. The worst thing for a parent is not being able to control or protect your own daughter. How do you sleep when your thirteen year-old is out on the streets somewhere? You question yourself: 'Is it something I've done? Have I treated her different to my other children?' But then the police told me how the grooming process works.

X: These lads have fast cars.

X: They're young…

X: … and good looking.

X: They get the girls into their cars by offering them vodka…

X: … some loud music…

X: … and a bit of a drive.

GEMMA: The girls may say 'no' one night

JESS: … but another night they might have had a bit of cider

JESS AND GEMMA: and say…

X: 'Yes'.

GEMMA AND JESS: That's when it starts. They get alcohol…

X: … and presents…

JESS AND GEMMA: *(Excited.)*… especially mobile phones. They call the girls…

X: 'Princess'

JESS AND GEMMA: … and make them feel special.

X: Then a few spliffs…

X: … and before they know it…

X: … they pass the girls on to older men.

X: The older men introduce the girls to…

X: … Class A drugs.

X: The girls become reliant on the men…

X: … and the drugs.

X: The men are seen to be fun…

X: … so they're the good ones…

X: … and the family are bad.

MARY: The parents are made to look like they just want to keep the girl in and make her life miserable. But it becomes more sinister because then it's payback time.

The girls are violently thrown to the floor.

X: Drugs cost… drugs cost money.

They hit the girls.

JESS AND GEMMA: They send the girls to pinch things.

X: The girls are passed around…

X: … the men might threaten to…

GEMMA: … smash up my house

JESS: … and rape my mum.

MARY: They rule. There is…

X: … no escape.

MARY: At first I didn't want anyone to know. I felt ashamed that she was involved but after the police had been here so often, I realised it wasn't about shame. It was about a young girl, a child, being exploited. I wanted these men caught, locked up. The law seemed powerless to protect my daughter. I called social services. I begged for help. They put Jess in a foster home round the corner. Every night I'd get a text from her foster carer saying she wasn't home. Again, it was me out looking for her so I asked for her to be moved out of county. I went to my local MP.

"If you don't, I fear I'll find her dead in a gutter? I want something done! If you don't, I'll go to the papers!" Within weeks, social services found her a therapeutic foster care place out of county.

I couldn't have asked for a better placement but, after a week and a half, two men abducted her. She was missing for a couple of days before she was found... with Gemma. Jess alleged she was hit with an iron bar by one man and chose to testify.

Two men were charged with supplying a Class A drug, detaining a child without lawful authority, and having sex with a child under the age of sixteen.

People think things like this only happen to 'bad' families but it can happen to anybody. These girls are victims of criminal acts: you are not to blame and nor are they. It's these men who are to blame. They've taken her innocence.

I am scared what my actions will be if these men get let off. I will go off my head. She's got problems in her head – big ones... recently threats of suicide...

JESS: Mum you don't know what it's like. I don't want to be here.

MARY: I was frightened she would do something.

JESS: *(Underscores the following words by singing the following.)*

Boys and girls come out to play,
The moon does shine as bright as day;
Come with a hoop, and come with a call,
Come with a good will or not at all.
Loose your supper, and loose your sleep,
Come to your playfellows in the street;
Up the ladder and down the wall.
A halfpenny loaf will serve us all.

MARY: She was singing nursery rhymes and getting all the stuff out from when she was little. She had her majorettes medal round her neck.

JESS: I want to die with this medal on. It was my favourite time!

X: There are loopholes in the law.

X: Sex with someone under sixteen is illegal.

X: But prosecution relies on the testimony of the child.

X: In practice when a child is over thirteen she has to testify.

X: The men know that.

X: They groom the girls to have sex with them as they turn thirteen.

X: The girls are too frightened to give evidence…

X: … or don't always fully understand that they were groomed…

X: … and that these men…

X: … were not real boyfriends.

The singing stops suddenly as **MARY** *breaks into her speech.*

MARY: I want to put a stop to this, that's why I'm speaking out. No one warned me that these lads drive round in their posh cars playing loud music grooming girls, and I didn't warn my daughter.
I want other parents to be aware.

BEX: The two men, aged thirty-one and forty-seven who abducted Jessica pleaded guilty to all charges.

MARY: They were sentenced to imprisonment of five years and eight months each but would probably be released after only two years.

JESS: With dependency issues remaining, Jessica remains a vulnerable target.

Section Ten

FINALLY SUCCESS...

PHIL: We had three months left…

BEX: Eighty-four days to be precise Phil…

PHIL: … and another 700,000 signatures to get. We're not even halfway yet!

RUTH: *(Enters excitedly.)* "Delirious?" have just called…

PHIL: A rock band. They did a gig in Mumbai… was just an idea… to get some interest from other parts of the world.

RUTH: Shot in the dark eh Phil?

PHIL: Worth a try.

RUTH: Certainly was.

PHIL: What's happened?

RUTH: 200,000 people signed…

BEX: 200,000?

RUTH: Yes! *(Celebration.)* That's not all. They played in Columbia last night and did the same thing! 400,000 signatures!

BEX AND PHIL: Yes!

PHIL: In the remaining eighty-three days *(**BEX** smiles.)* the team came within sight of their target. We collected petitions from every continent through:

BEX: Signed postcards;

RUTH: Thumb prints;

PHIL: Freedom walls;

BEX: Website sign ups;

PHIL: Football events;

RUTH: …a Watford player had been trafficked so they asked fans to text in.

PHIL: With just over 100,000 signatures to get and only… *(Looks at **BEX**.)*

BEX: … eight days Phil.

PHIL: Eight days to go…we tried to get in touch with a Nigerian church network.

RUTH: *(To the team.)* We can't be having a voice on behalf of other people and not include Africa… Africa has to have a voice!

*The team takes heed of **RUTH**'s advice and sets to work trying to contact that community.*

RUTH: *(Addressing the audience.)* At the time, I think there was a gathering every month where people would literally travel on foot far to listen to the sermon.

*The office-staff join **RUTH**'s address.*

BEX: We were right up against our deadline…

RUTH: Our hearts were pounding…

PHIL: This was a mass gathering in a country where trafficking is… well prolific!

BEX: We waited for their response.

PHIL: … and waited…

RUTH: … waited…

BEX: … three days to go!

ALL: … waited…

PHIL: … for news.

STEVE: Guys… we have news.

PHIL, RUTH AND BEX: Well?

STEVE: I think you should sit down.

RUTH: Just tell us!

STEVE: You need to sit down.

PHIL: Have they said no? If they say no we're done! There's nothing else to do… no one else we can go to!

STEVE: They gathered hundreds of thousands of Africans in this church service, as far as the eye could see. The leader explained that "We were STOP THE TRAFFIK, we are going to stop the traffik and would you stand up if you prevent it." And they all stood up, one by one, the footage was amazing!

PHIL, RUTH AND BEX: What?

STEVE: They're all signing.

RUTH: In the end we had one and a half million signatures!

BEX: And a platform to deliver them at the UN's first Global Initiative to fight traffiking!

    BEX *and* **PHIL** *exit celebrating.*

RUTH: Steve spoke at that event, alongside Ricky Martin, and I'm telling you… Steve was better. He preached the sermon of his life. It was just brilliant, calling the world to not be apathetic.

STEVE: The UN recognised that STOP THE TRAFFIK has relationships with people around the world… when people act things change.

The scene below is played out in silhouette behind a screen that the cast has set up.

RUTH: We had this most amazing young woman who had come to us. She first rang STOP THE TRAFFIK's office as our number came up when she searched it. She'd been trafficked and talked to Bex. She became part of our STOP THE TRAFFIK family, sharing and learning together. She came and shared the stage as we delivered that petition onstage. She then got asked by the executive director, to meet with her. She spent an hour sharing her story with him. He listened. He was moved. He learnt. When Steve and I were on our way to the airport, Emily, Steve's daughter phoned. She was still at the conference, and she shouted down the phone: "They've signed the agreement" and they'd made Steve the UN Special Advisor on Community Action Against Trafficking. So we got to the airport in Vienna, and…I danced on the coffee table!

Everyone celebrates as they take down the screen revealing the trafficked characters.

BEX: Everyone who signed made a difference…

PHIL: …and will continue to.

KIRI: Kiri's story is evidence of this.

VERONICA: And Veronicas.

JESSICA: And Jessicas.

PHIL: Let's hope it's still possible to rescue…

SUNNI: … Sunni…

WHINNEY: … and Whinney.

COJO: Remember Cojo…

YAO: … and his friend Yao.

X: Always think what sort of chocolate you are buying… you choose!

COJO: If you don't… you are buying something Cojo and his friends suffered to make.

X: Trafficking starts in the community and ends in the community…

ALL: … our community.

> **RUTH** *and* **BEX** *address the audience as* **STEVE** *and* **PHIL** *organise the rest of the cast to create a human pyramid to reach a key that has been hanging high, centre stage and unnoticed, the whole time.*

RUTH: So what next? I think we've just gotta get ourselves organised because what's grown is, like, everything. And that's what I mean about the snowflakes, that was the right message then, but actually, when you get a trillion snowflakes and everything is…that, that only works if everybody in some way is co-ordinated.

BEX: And, the problem with our existence is people are competitive. We're only ever gunna get ahead of the traffikers if we can predict it. The prediction power of technology is amazing. You know there's the frailty of it but if we begin to see the migration patterns around the world, climate changes, the move of where people are going to be vulnerable, if we can then predict and get ahead of them, we can start to build that sort of resilience into people. We need to make the trafficking business unprofitable.

RUTH: On the other hand technology is the tool, globally, that has enabled trafficking to thrive. And we have to work globally… I call it 'glocal', we have to connect the two, network globally, lead locally.

PHIL: The choices we all make allow traffiking to continue… if it's cheap, you'll buy it… who cares whether somebody is trafficked or not. It's by closing our eyes and choosing to accept it that traffiking continues.

If you ask questions and act on the answers then maybe we've got a chance to stop it.

BEX: Everyone's talking about saving the planet, and it's funny, the planet doesn't need saving, the planet will save itself, in the end.

RUTH: It's the people that actually need to get it right: what we do and how we treat each other. And I honestly felt, when I looked around all these actors, the Intelligence Agencies, governments, business, banks and every community anywhere and everywhere – none of us can do this on our own, none of us, but we all have a role to play. We need to find a way to shine a light on this global criminal business and see how it works.

If we can see it, we can stop it together.

End.

Salamander Street

Teachers – if you are interested in buying a set of texts for your class please email info@salamanderstreet.com – we would be happy to discuss discounts and keep you up to date with our latest publications and study guides.

Follow us on Twitter or Facebook or visit our website for the latest news.

www.ingramcontent.com/pod-product-compliance
Lightning Source LLC
Jackson TN
JSHW011655231224
75956JS00004B/35